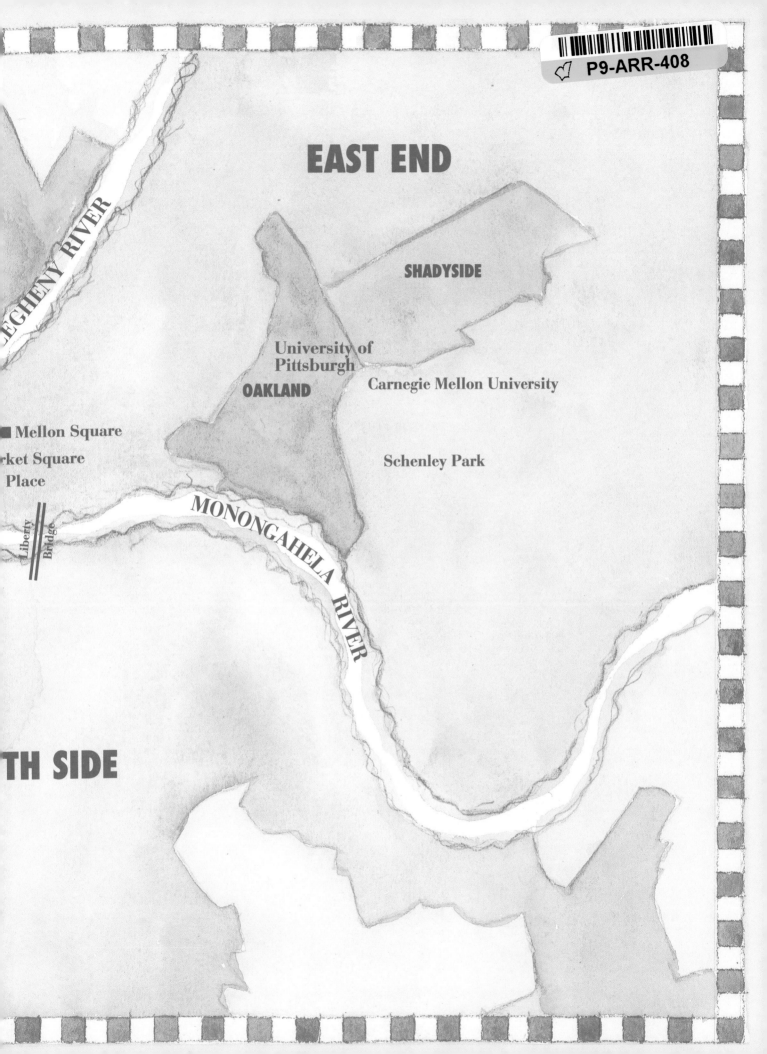

EAST END

SHADYSIDE

ALLEGHENY RIVER

University of
Pittsburgh

OAKLAND

Carnegie Mellon University

Schenley Park

Mellon Square

rket Square
Place

Liberty
Bridge

MONONGAHELA RIVER

TH SIDE

PITTSBURGH

Pittsburgh
Text © 1997 by Ruth Hoover Seitz
Photography © 1997 by Blair Seitz
ISBN 1879441-96-9
Library of Congress Catalog Card Number 96-68405

Published by

RB
BOOKS
"...richly beautiful"

Seitz and Seitz, Inc.
1006 N. Second St.
Harrisburg, Pa 17102-3121
717-232-7944

Graphic Design by Klinginsmith & Company
Printed in Hong Kong

PREVIOUS PAGE: Sunset warms the lighted spires of PPG
Place, a corporate showcase in Pittsburgh's Downtown.
THIS PAGE: The sun rises over the city of Pittsburgh as
viewed from Mt. Washington.

PITTSBURGH

RUTH HOOVER SEITZ • PHOTOGRAPHY BY BLAIR SEITZ

RB
BOOKS
"...richly beautiful"

Harrisburg, PA

FOREWORD BY MYRON COPE

FOREWORD
BY MYRON COPE

An acclaimed broadcast journalist and book author, Myron Cope is known for his colorful analyses of Pittsburgh Steelers football games on WTAE.

Through a fairly lengthy writing career, I was asked from time to time by my magazine editors quartered in New York, "Well, when are you moving to New York? You'll be offered book contracts just by visiting the right bars." In subsequent years as a Pittsburgh sportscaster, larger broadcast markets telephoned. But never did it cross my mind to leave the city where I had been born.

Why risk happiness? In Pittsburgh I was happy.

For all her faults (and what city does not have many?), Pittsburgh's hills and rivers and generally unpretentious people add up to a place hard to leave. One of our problems is a disproportionately aging population. I share the blame. We elderly, by the thousands, simply do not care to go elsewhere.

Out-of-state journalists, whether visiting Pittsburgh or speaking from afar, to this day sometimes invoke Pittsburgh's old moniker–The Smokey City. Are they just ignorant or blind as well? Smoke-control laws adopted shortly after World War II scrubbed Pittsburgh clean of her steel-mill soot. The view from restaurants atop Mt. Washington is more dazzling than any I have found atop San Francisco's hills.

But enough defensiveness. I'll just say I'm here for the duration.

INTRODUCTION

When a Rand McNally survey named Pittsburgh the nation's most livable city, my husband, Blair Seitz, and I went there to write and photograph a feature for a European syndicate.

Pittsburgh first beguiled us with its alluring cityscapes. Watching fireworks over Three Rivers Stadium from Mt. Washington etched an unforgettable downtown panorama on our memories. Also, the beauty of the green hills was as palpable as the warmth of the people. Pittsburgh was indeed "a city," as *Travel and Leisure* Magazine noted, "where people go home to their parents for Sunday dinner."

We promised ourselves more delving into this City's bright pallette of attractions. We returned with our children for the Three Rivers Arts Festival and also for a theatre weekend.

Later, during a winter visit, we explored a range of dining options—Indian curries on Craig Street, fish sandwiches in the Strip District, and entreés with a view from the Top of the Triangle. We learned that former residents return for such favorites as the almond torte at Prantl's in Shadyside and chicken soup at Rhoda's in Squirrel Hill.

Over the subsequent months of exploring and researching to prepare this book, we came under the spell of Pittsburgh's big-city attractions and local idiosyncrasies. We were grateful for the generous assistance given by the Pittsburgh Convention and Visitors Bureau and for architectural information explained by the Pittsburgh History & Landmarks Foundation. We appreciated the willingness of organizations to review facts and the faithful attentiveness of our editors, especially Millie Rinehart. Most of all, we thank the people of Pittsburgh who invited us—even momentarily—into their lives.

–*Ruth Hoover Seitz*

CONTENTS

CHAPTER

1   AMIDST RIVERS AND HILLS... 6

2   THE GOLDEN TRIANGLE TO ITS GLISTENING POINT.............. 28

3   ARTS ENSHRINED AND THE SCIENCES ADVANCED.................. 54

4   A CITY OF FAMILY NEIGHBORHOODS.................................... 84

5   IN PITTSBURGH AND BEYOND..114

AMIDST HILLS AND RIVERS

Pittsburgh possesses two kinds of beauty–the noble buildings designed by its architects and, beneath its urban skin, a terrain endowed by the earth itself millions of years ago. The varied topography offers height for perspective and rocky depth for road tunnels. As a bonus, two rivers merge and create a third, their watery flow softening the angles of Pittsburgh's hills.

From the 62d floor of the USX Building, it is easy to mentally erase the architecture of the Triangle and to visualize the natural features that captivated Pulitzer prizewinner Annie Dillard in her writings about her childhood city. "I see only those forested mountains and hills, and the way the rivers lie flat and moving among them, and the way the low land lies wooded among them, and the blunt mountains rise in darkness from the rivers' banks, steep from the rugged south and rolling from the north. . . . "

With the highest elevation 600 feet above the "flats" bordering the rivers, Pittsburgh's hills rise and dip randomly and sometimes precipitiously for humans. No longer newcomers but hardly natives, my husband Blair and I were scouting Pittsburgh one afternoon. Our car descended a steep grade in Lawrenceville. The street was also uncommonly narrow–probably because it could be no wider–and without warning, our side mirror scrunched against the one on a delivery van going *up* the hill. Residents have assured me that such hazards also befall them. It was "Jamie" D. VanTrump, co-founder of the Pittsburgh History & Landmarks Foundation, who referred to the lay of the land as "turbulent topography."

Those hills, they do leave an impression. They become a subconscious but integral factor in the daily lives of residents. Explains one West Ender, "When I look over to the Overlook from my hill, I can see half the world, and I love it!" The hills seem to imprint the psyche of a Pittsburgher with an extra portion of spunk or determination, that

character trait that defies constraints such as a winter snowfall that averages forty-two inches.

Pittsburghers consider a street on a seventy-degree angle a grade, not a hill. Hilltops provide lookouts to engage in romance and reflection. Each Pittsburgher returns to a favorite vantage point, perhaps West End Overlook or Riverview Park, to see the fireworks. The mountainous ups and downs create challenging sports events such as the toughest single day cyling in North America, the Thrift Drug Classic Elite Men's Race, which tests bicyclists in a grueling 108-mile urban course with eleven climbs up Sycamore Street to Mt. Washington. Those hilly streets build finely structured legs, rope-taut from uphill striding. To illustrate this, one city book that came out in the mini-skirt era of the 1970s published photos of local legs.

The hills have dominated Pittsburgh's building patterns. Rowhouses with high front steps have squeezed against each other since early immigrants piled into Pittsburgh during industry's boom. Hilltops shoulder bridges that span ravines and join neighborhoods. Concrete steps shimmy up hillsides, and two inclines smoothly glide up and down Mt. Washington.

It was the construction of the first incline, the Monongahela, in 1870 that fueled the desire for workers at the factories below to live on Mt. Washington. Inclines became a fixture for residents who built along the back slopes. Consequently, this neighborhood was shocked when a sign posted on Thanksgiving Day 1962 announced that the Duquesne Incline would be closed for lack of repair funds, perhaps permanently.

Emotional attachment aroused some 5,000 residents who counted on the Incline–if only for an emergency return from work during a snowstorm. A door-to-door canvass developed into negotiations with the owners to establish the neighborhood's right to operate a piece of their history. The

> *"In the rolling country that encompasses the city with ravine and wooded slope, there still remain gentle loveliness and restfulness in impressive contrast with the throbbing industry of town."*
>
> **Charles Mulford Robinson,** *Pittsburgh Survey,* **1908**

community organized fundraisers as simple as bake sales and $1 souvenir tickets. Money trickled in with only one sizable anonymous contribution that arrived after Helen Clay Frick had come by for an incline ride. The upshot is that since it reopened July 1, 1963, the Duquesne Incline has functioned as a non-profit corporation, transporting passengers seven days a week. According to the Port Authority of Allegheny County, this incline is the only public transit facility in the United States that operates without government subsidy.

The reality behind that statistic is the tireless volunteerism of retirees Ruth and David Miller, who remember riding the Pittsburgh inclines to college classes and who now devote full-time energy to managing the Duquesne. Their payoff is that Pittsburghers and out-of-towners can experience a brush with this City's past but with a spectacular view of its present.

Pittsburgh stands majestically in relief, a fifty-five square-mile city sculpture. Like any three-dimensional work of art, the City is transformed by light variations. At twilight from a condominium on Grandview Avenue while Blair was photographing, I watched the multi-colored shapes of corporate Pittsburgh recede into deep blue dusk, and lights of fewer colors gradually illuminate the windows of skyscrapers until the cityscape glowed and twinkled with its own magical dimensions.

Height *is* magic. Pittsburgh's overlooks spark memory sifting. So many of the times that I peered down from a hilltop, my eyes immediately spotted Point State Park, Pittsburgh's gateway between the Monongahela and the Allegheny rivers. A spacious green park closed to traffic, the Point is serene and calming, the result of three decades of intense discussion about the use of Pittsburgh's most important piece of real estate.

Two centuries earlier this tongue of land was a point of contention between the area's first European settlers. In 1753 from McKees Rocks, an Indian mound on the south bank of the Ohio, young George Washington determined that the Point would be an ideal site to build a fort from which to control the disputed area we now call Western Pennsylvania. The next year the French ousted the English and began constructing their own Fort Duquesne on the same location.

Four years later when British General John Forbes marched west, forging a land route with 6,000 troops, the French burned and abandoned their fort prior to his arrival. The English reclaimed this pivotal Point; named it "Pittsburgh" after William Pitt, Great Britain's prime minister; and enlarged Fort Pitt, a stockade with five bastions, to gain control of the three rivers that promised an opening to the West.

And so began the era of westward migration. In the single year of 1788, the Ohio River carried 18,000 pioneers into its valley and beyond. Although the fort lost its significance after the Revolution, the town of Pittsburgh mushroomed. Here merchants and traders provisioned pioneers heading west. At first flatboats and then later barges pushed by sternwheel steamboats transported goods for the new settlers.

Today Pittsburgh conveys openness despite its irregular topography. From a high point, I have enjoyed a bird's eye view of streets and structures that I had experienced closeup. I have looked down at the PPG Place, for instance, and recalled that the day before I had sat in the Plaza surrounded by the structure's mirroring and had enjoyed a noontime concert and a classic car display.

From West End Overlook, the rivers thread through the City, adding value to the landscape and to the business world. In the early nineteenth century, the Allegheny River served loggers and oil drillers by carrying their goods on its 325-mile course from the New York border to the Ohio at Pittsburgh. Sandstone and lubricants are still among the cargo hauled by tow barges. From East Brady in Armstrong County south to the tip of the Triangle, barges utilize the Allegheny's system of eight locks and dams built by the United States Army Corps of Engineers.

Pleasure boaters traveling a stretch of the River also "lock through." As the number of public docks increases, residents launch from and stay in one area for skiing or fishing. Kayakers and scullers often take advantage of the sheltered flow of the Allegheny in the back channel of Herr Island, now known as Washington's Landing.

The Three Rivers Rowing Center, built on the Island's north shore in the late eighties, accommodates spectators and training equipment for area rowing teams. From the 30th Street Bridge, I saw high school teams muscle upriver, the clear calls of their coxswains blending with sideline cheers on an autumn Sunday. In the distance, a dark rain cloud pierced by the spire of Polish Hill's Immaculate Heart of Mary Church intensified the beauty of the sleek boats with their rhythmic movement. Pittsburgh's rivers are more stunning because of the hills around them. On his first visit filmmaker Steven Spielberg praised the City's "spectacular sets, all ready to go."

Before it joins the Allegheny to form the Ohio River, the "Mon" flows 129 miles north from Fairmont, West Virginia. Nine locks and dams create a navigation channel deep enough for ocean-going vessels. Ever since coal was discovered in its surrounding hills, the Monongahela has figured significantly as an industrial waterway. Transporting goods by barge costs less per ton than by rail or by truck. Pittsburgh is the country's largest inland waterway port, shipping over a million tons of cargo to/from the Gulf of Mexico to reach international markets. The Rivers are a timeless commercial highway.

Pittsburgh's bridges of varying designs give the Three Rivers City distinction. With its 573 bridges–twenty-two cross rivers–Pittsburgh could be called America's City of Bridges. The only city in the world with more is Venice, according to the narrator on the Gateway Clipper boat cruise.

Pittsburgh boasts several remarkable approaches. Tunnels, bridges, inclines, and the world's shortest subway known as "The T" transport commuters and visitors from all directions into Pittsburgh. Each entrance guarantees a notable view. In addition to churches and houses layering the slopes, architecturally interesting bridges span the three rivers. Each route unfurls at least one rewarding cityscape. Built in the 1880s, the Smithfield Street Bridge, lenticular or lens-shaped, carries arrivals from the South Side across the "Mon." Some of this span's traffic pours out of the Liberty Tubes which tunnel through Mt. Washington. The 6th, 7th and 9th Street bridges, three identical self-anchored suspension spans painted a lively "Aztec gold," cross the Allegheny north of the Point.

My favorite route into Pennsylvania's second largest city runs east from the airport, a state-of-the-art depot.

Rolling through the Fort Pitt Tunnels, I all at once shoot into daylight again with the cityscape gleaming beyond the Fort Pitt Bridge. Of the seven bridges crossing the Monongahela to the Triangle, Fort Pitt is the closest to the Point–and the busiest. Its two decks carry more than 140,000 vehicles each day. For me, this view of the Downtown confirms my arrival in a city of significance.

While bridges are a signature of the region's rivers, parks are an important land element. Twenty percent of the City's acreage remains natural and wild with parks in Pittsburgh and surrounding Allegheny County meeting varied interests. For example, Beechwood Farms features equestrian trails, and people flock to Flagstaff Hill on summer evenings for free outdoor films. Schenley Park's ice skating rink has been a long-time favorite winter site. Wrapping around Pittsburgh, the Three Rivers Heritage Trail, a park for biking and hiking along the riverbanks, was planned as a link to a regional greenway. The City's verdancy rates highly with residents. One transport from Cleveland says, "Pittsburgh sits so pretty like a green bowl."

Beyond the limits of this park-rich city, natural wilds come close to urban development. Seeing deer is commonplace during the twenty-five-minute commute from woodsy Bridgeville and even within residential areas in Oakland. However, bear sightings usually occur farther afield in Butler County about twenty miles from the city limits.

In Pittsburgh's Oakland neighborhood, a hub for tens of thousands of college students, is Schenley Park, a rolling terrain with trails that can enclose joggers in forested wilds. Its vegetation is one of Pittsburgh's three assets, according to Patrick Horsbrugh, an architect who analyzed the City's potential in 1963. He wrote, "The quality and character of the City of Pittsburgh depend upon the remarkable combination of water, of topography formed by that water, and of the vegetation sustained by that water, all that is collectively known as the *landscape*." Without question, the beauty of Pittsburgh originates in its rivers and hills.

PAGE 7: Aerial view from west shows Pittsburgh's Downtown, the Golden Triangle rimmed by rivers, their bridges, and hilly neighborhoods.
PAGE 9: The Smithfield Bridge is the City's oldest span.
LEFT: From Arlington Avenue on the South Side, residences line Pittsburgh's steep hillsides against the backdrop of the corporate skyline.
ABOVE: According to locals, houses along such precipitous terrain as West End's Lakewood Street are situated on a grade, not a hill.

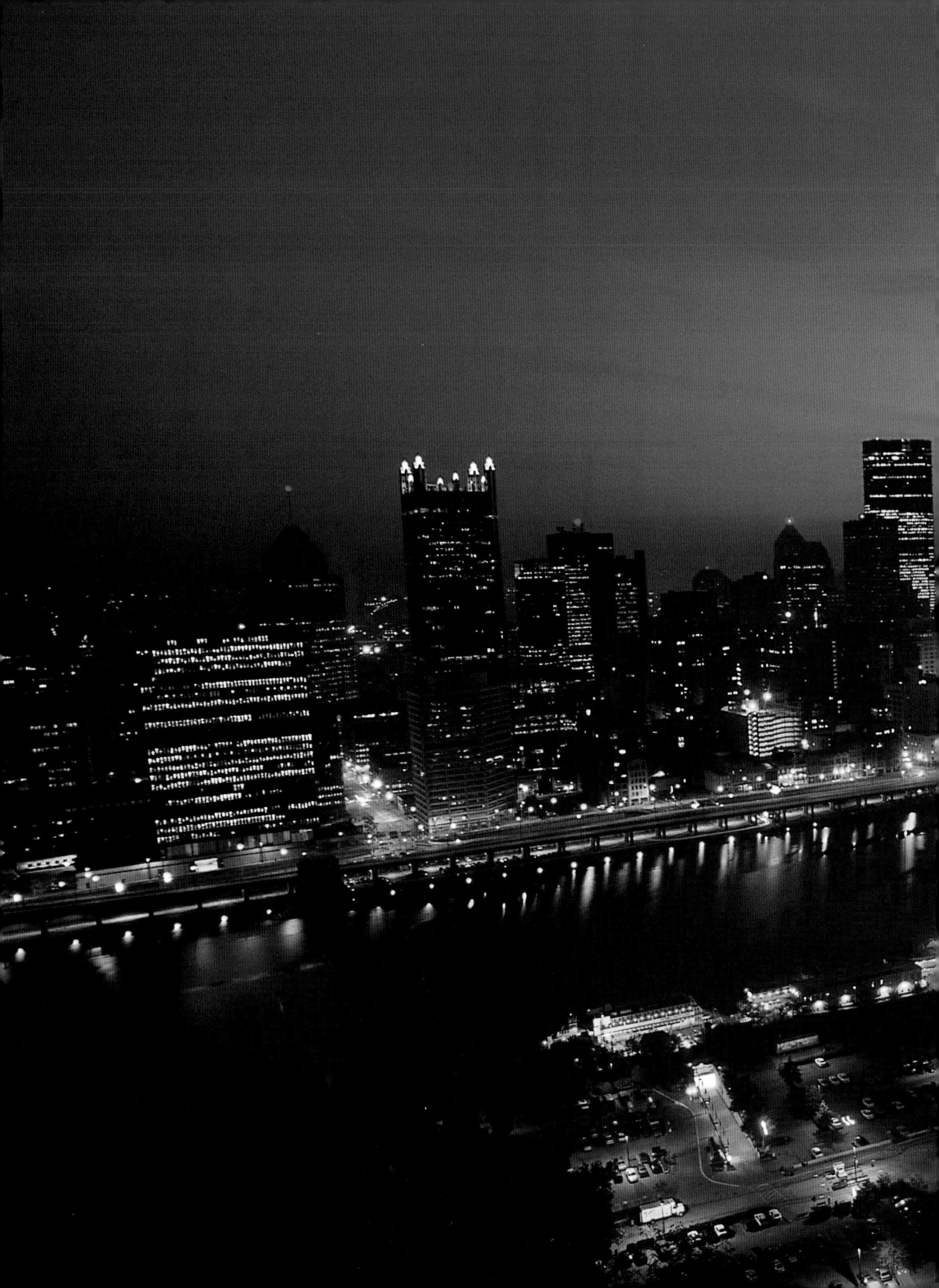

PREVIOUS PAGES: From Mt. Washington, a sunrise highlights Pittsburgh on both sides of the Monongahela River with Station Square, a restored shopping-dining complex, on the South Side.

LEFT: The downtown skyline from the 6th Street Bridge across the Allegheny River is as stunning as from the 7th and 9th Street bridges which mirror each other in color and style.

ABOVE: A Fort Pitt Museum exhibit illustrates Pittsburgh's significance as a trading post.

TOP LEFT: Pittsburgh's topography offers dramatic cityscapes such as this sunset view from a condominium on Mt. Washington, which is 600 feet above the rivers.

LEFT: Route 376, a major artery into the City from the east, also provides easy entrance to Oakland.

ABOVE: Night views of Pittsburgh's stunning skyline lure people to the West End Overlook for picnics, fireworks, and photography.

PREVIOUS PAGES: Racers in the Thrift Drug Classic Elite Men's competition climb Sycamore Street to the peak of Mt. Washington, a route with an elevation gain of about 350 feet in less than a mile.

ABOVE: Twenty percent of Pittsburgh terrain is set aside as park land, where residents relax as in West Park on the city's North Side.

RIGHT: An historic Pittsburgh transportation mode, the Duquesne Incline gives residents and tourists a scenic ride up Mt. Washington.

ABOVE: Fall foliage intensifies the beauty of Pittsburgh's cityscapes, here from Spring Hill Cemetery looking south.

RIGHT: In the 476 acres of Frick Park, paths give lovers of the outdoors, including those in wheelchairs, access to dense woods.

"How inexhaustible is the local landscape, how mysterious, how wonderful! From my long love, how can I cease to praise! The streets rise and the streets descend. Who knows where they lead?"

James D. Van Trump, co-founder, Pittsburgh History & Landmarks Foundation

TOP LEFT: A tow barge, the most economical means of freight transport, travels the Allegheny River under the Fort Duquesne Bridge.

LEFT: Spanning the Ohio River a mile down from the Point, the West End Bridge, a graceful tied arch bridge, frames the downtown at dawn.

ABOVE: The 6th Street Bridge across the Allegheny leads to the downtown from the North Side.

NEXT PAGES: High schoolers sweep row on the Allegheny River. They launch from the Three Rivers Rowing Center, which serves area rowers as did twenty boathouses a century ago.

THE GOLDEN TRIANGLE TO ITS GLISTENING POINT

Poised for the 21st century, Pittsburgh's downtown is an urban phoenix. In stages it has succeeded in changing from a smoky, grimy workhorse to a pleasant, convenient business hub. Its rebirth stems from two major development programs. The first was Renaissance I, essentially a cleanup launched in the 1940s, and the second was Renaissance II, a building surge that modernized Pittsburgh's skyline. Each day 115,000 commuters descend on the peninsula that points westward towards the Ohio River and that lies between the Allegheny and the Monogahela rivers. Their destination, the Downtown, is known as the Golden Triangle.

Pittsburgh's downtown is golden in several respects.

Its 255 acres contain a dense concentration of business and property wealth. The downtown's market value soars into the billions, with the spacing of its real estate conveying airiness in spite of its compactness. It *looks* golden. At dusk from Mt. Washington, the southern face of the Triangle is an alluring cityscape, its buildings glowing in the sun and the window lights sparkling like diamond chips.

Among the skyscrapers that readily denote Pittsburgh is PPG Place, a Gothic rendition of reflective glass and headquarters for Pittsburgh Plate Glass Industries. PPG's decision to place in its home city this crown jewel ushered in the 1980s building surge of Renaissance II. Home of Pennsylvania Blue Shield, Fifth Avenue Place turns its face of glass and brass to welcome new arrivals through the Gateway. Its red-tipped needle and lotus-shaped tower penetrate the skyline. The USX Tower, Pittsburgh's tallest building, has an exposed frame constructed of Cor-Ten weathering steel, a product of United States Steel, the company that helped to make Pittsburgh the Steel Capital of the World. From the beacon tower on the Grant Building, a light blinks "P I T T S B U R G H" in Morse code. One Oxford Centre, a sleek forty-six-story structure of twin aluminum and glass octagons, adds gleam to the skyline.

The architectural variety of the Golden Triangle heightens its interest. Architects have restored older structures and designed contemporary ones that complement each other. The 1836 Burke Building, the oldest downtown commercial building and a survivor of the 1845 fire, now stands alongside the mirrored fantasy of PPG Place. On Fort Pitt Boulevard remains a concentration of nineteenth century buildings that once served riverboat traffic along the Monongahela shorefront. In the Boulevard's 200 block the stone facades, cast iron fronts, arched windows, and ornamental gables of three to five-story buildings add a unique texture to the riverfront.

Among the many other buildings dating from the City's industrial heyday are several banks that symbolize the financial growth of the "gilded age." On 4th Street inside the Bank Tower winds a stunning spiral stairwell. The ornate entranceway of the Dollar Bank with its watchful lions dominates the block.

Lions also guard the Grant Street entrance to the Allegheny County Courthouse and Jail Annex. Joined by the Bridge of Sighs, these two structures designed by Paris-trained Henry Hobson Richardson are considered world-class, and even near-perfect by some architects.

Station Square, a South Side commercial complex with a restored rail terminal at its heart, seems to extend the Downtown across the Monongahela. Tourists frequently leave the Square's stores and restaurants, travel through the Victorian-style portals of the City's oldest bridge, the Smithfield, to return to the Triangle on a route that leads to several of the downtown's public parks.

Mellon Square, a plaza with underground parking, welcomes noontime camaraderie. This Square is a central oasis of greenery and fountains for surrounding office buildings such as the Alcoa Building, a thirty-floor structure made of aluminum panels; Three Mellon Bank Center, a bank with Italian marble columns and an office tower; and the Union Trust Building, an edifice with ornate terra cotta dormers designed by local architect Frederick Osterling. The Square provides park space for the Westin William Penn Hotel, which has been restored to the 1916 sumptuousness planned by its creator, Henry Clay Frick. Today a harpist plays in the Palm Court Lobby at teatime. In this grand hotel, a young Lawrence Welk once thrilled Pittsburgh audiences with his Champagne Music Makers and their bubble machine.

Another noon and happy hour favorite is Market Square, a colorful setting with robust traditions. The storefronts with flower boxes along lantern-lit Market Place resemble an Alpine village. In eateries and piano bars, the sandwiches and beverages are as hearty as the spirit of the servers at a corner landmark, the 1870 Original Oyster House. Summer happenings on the Square are well publicized, but one July noon it was surprising to hear a town crier read out the news, a practice that began during an extended newspaper strike in 1992.

Workers in the Central Business District also flock to the indoor PPG Food Court. After buying from vendors, they rendezvous at central tables in an area designed for the lunch crowd.

Downtown has long been and still is a favorite of shoppers. "You can't walk more than five blocks without seeing somebody you know," explained one sixty-year-old who frequents the Triangle for its stores and cultural events. "I'll meet you by Kaufmann's clock" has been a familiar arrangement for years. Underground parking accommodates loyal patrons of boutiques and department stores.

The Downtown's six churches serve worshippers from local workplaces and from the wider metropolitan area as well as from the community condominiums such as Gateway Towers.

To avoid curbside building, a downtown planning policy promotes plaza space and spacious entrances. When employees want to stretch beyond the Downtown's compactness, they head west past flowering beds near Fort Pitt Boulevard to Point State Park and its dazzling fountain.

The Point is Pittsburgh's downtown playground. During the work week, the open lawn and shade trees of Point State Park invite lunchtime relaxation– fishing, jogging, chatting, or munching on *sammitches*, as Pittsburghers say. To the sound of a fountain that jets water more than 200 feet from a natural underground reservoir, visitors are recharged by the relaxed atmosphere of the Park.

The expansive lawn of the Point is particularly fitting for Pittsburgh's Three Rivers Regatta, a summer festival with a stunning variety of events. The program boasts waterski stunts, balloon launches, powerboat races, and small plane acrobatics. On water, in the air or across land, Pittsburghers engage in this annual frolic with typical Pittsburgh zest.

When I attended, enthusiasm ran high even during the Regatta's early morning balloon launch. By dawn, a few colorful balloons were already aloft, following a south wind over the Monongahela River. In an open area, clusters of people surrounded the billowing fabric of partially inflated balloons. One ground crew was holding open the envelope of a balloon shaped like a battery, while the burner shot the hot flame that would heat the air to inflate the fabric.

With Pittsburgh ranked as the third most challenging American city for balloonists, just behind Atlanta and Philadelphia, it is understandable that the Hot Air Balloon Classic annually draws world-experienced pilots to the City's Regatta. Some drift in with logs of 5,000 or more hours, eager to add some more hours in this challenging airspace. Launching from the Point, pilots covet a current that will lift their balloons high enough to clear the City and then move them far beyond buildings to a sizable open site for landing.

An expert balloonist informed a crowd of spectators that balloons can't really race because they depend on wind for their speed. Those with unusual shapes are more difficult to launch than round ones, and because they take up more space, they are more challenging to land.

During the day, the action on the rivers features other events. Water skiers perform stunts. Sternwheelers compete. Power boats race up to 140 mph between the

6th Street Bridge and the submarine docked on the Ohio River. Hilariously dressed employee groups launch inventive vessels in the "Anything That Floats" competition and join the Wet Bottom Club when their contraptions sink. Laughter and teasing attest to that enthusiastic spirit of Western Pennsylvanians.

Each June during the Three Rivers Arts Festival, corporations exhibit art in their public spaces. Foyers, plazas, and parks feature contemporary visual and performing arts. From booths erected in the shadows of the Gateway Center buildings, artists from across the country market their fine crafts. On more than a half dozen stages, singers, instrumentalists, drama troupes, and dancers entertain audiences with familar and innovative interpretations.

Outdoor festivities on the Point were developed only after pollutants had been removed from Pittsburgh's water and air. The history of Pittsburgh's cleanup is a story that spans several decades and that describes the Point's transformation as the aesthetic focus of the Downtown.

Steady industrial production since the Civil War had layered the city with grime and smoke. In 1938 plans emerged for a thirty-six-acre park and fort reconstruction on the Point, but World War II delayed them. By 1945 personal safeguards against air pollutants no longer worked. Double closet doors kept clothes clean inside the house, but it took two white shirts to get an executive through the business day. Derelict housing, traffic nightmares, sewage-strewn rivers, and freight discards on the Point were harrowing realities. To keep company headquarters in Pittsburgh, the City needed to redo the Gateway.

The Allegheny Conference, a distinctive partnership between government and business, figured prominently in the overhaul of Steel City. This committee's work launched Renaissance I. First came flood control measures and clean air guidelines that reduced pollutants by sixty-five percent.

Renewal progressed with the completion of the first three office buildings known as Gateway Center in 1953. Next followed the Gateway and Equitable Plazas and surrounding structures–the Hilton Hotel (1959), Gateway Four (1960), the United Steelworkers Building (1966), and Westinghouse headquarters (1970). That same year the Three Rivers Stadium rose on the North Side as the home of Pittsburgh's Steelers and Pirates. The Fort Pitt Museum was installed in a reconstructed bastion on the Point to honor the histori-

cal competition for this crucial triangle of land.

While the country watched this first American post-war venture into urban renewal, the Allegheny Conference worked tirelessly year after year. Each leader followed the protocol of attending the meetings in person, capitalizing on his vast experiences, and wielding his influence not only in Pittsburgh but also in Harrisburg and Washington, D.C. Key people such as Richard King Mellon and Mayor David Lawrence rose above political differences and worked productively with a team that included Wallace Richards, Park Martin and John Robin. After soliciting the advice of experts, they evaluated the best ideas, resolved their differences and accomplished an urban miracle.

In 1961 Pittsburgh unveiled the Civic Arena, a $22 million facility with a retractable dome roof that can open in two minutes to give concertgoers a special effect. Such legends as the Beatles and the Doors performed here, but hockey fans know the "Igloo," as the Arena is sometimes called, as home to the Pittsburgh Penguins, winners of the Stanley Cup. The residents of Crawford Square in the vicinty of the Arena can also enjoy a brisk twenty-minute walk to a play or concert in the Downtown's Cultural District.

Located in the Penn-Liberty area, the Cultural District encompasses a fourteen-block cluster of buildings set aside for exhibits and art performances. In the interest of nourishing a rich variety of performances, the Pittsburgh Cultural Trust provides for experimental theatre as well as grand opera. Blending funding sources, the Trust masterminds support for art events by planning for parking, shopping, dining and riverside strolling.

As a result of this strategic foresight, throngs depart from events at such grand restorations as Heinz Hall, the Benedum Center and the Byham Theatre and walk to restaurants and coffee bars for a late night repast. Gallery openings support area arts. A river breeze blows through curbside pear trees that bloom each spring. A two-tier park effectively utilizes the flood plain along the Allegheny.

With its smoky reputation cleaned up decades ago, the city of Pittsburgh is dynamic, its Downtown the Golden Triangle not only at sunset. Through each creative stage of development, the Triangle's growth from its Point to the Crosstown Boulevard is organic, a remarkable result of visionary urban planning and cooperative renewal efforts.

PAGES 30-31: Pittsburgh's evening lights grace the Monongahela River and Downtown.

PREVIOUS PAGES: Retailers in restored buildings do business on the edge of Market Square, which has been open space since the 1784 plan of Pittsburgh.

ABOVE: At plazas such as this one in the shadow of the USX Building, the Triangle's tallest skyscraper, workers relax over lunch.

TOP RIGHT: Pittsburgh zoning downtown provides for open landscaped areas such as Market Square.

RIGHT: A vendor sells lemonade at PPG Plaza, an outdoor setting with innumerable reflections.

"Pittsburgh moved ahead as quickly and daringly as it could with one all consuming objective in mind: to rescue the city from floods, smoke, and blight. Where else could a start be made but in the then fluttering, economic heart of a metropolitan area of two-million people downtown?"

David Lawrence (1889-1966), Pittsburgh's mayor during Renaissance I

GATEWAY CENTER

THE FIRST PUBLICLY SPONSORED
PRIVATELY FINANCED
URBAN REDEVELOPMENT PROJECT
IN THE UNITED STATES

OPENED IN 1952 BY

THE EQUITABLE

ABOVE: Fifth Avenue Place greets downtown arrivals via the Fort Duquesne Bridge, the city's gateway from the international airport.
TOP RIGHT: Mellon Square, a well-landscaped plaza one acre square, is a lunchtime retreat for workers in surrounding skyscrapers.
RIGHT: The bronze clock at Kaufmann's at the corner of Smithfield Street and Fifth Avenue is a downtown landmark for shoppers.

ABOVE: Facades of the historic Monongahela waterfront display architectural variety against the energy-efficient reflective glass curtainwalls of PPG Place, headquarters of PPG Industries.

RIGHT: The bustle along Smithfield Street illustrates a lively, compact downtown. Pedestrians can walk east-west across town in fifteen minutes.

ABOVE: Planned and built during Renaissance I, Equitable Plaza near Gateway Center provides shaded open space, an area used to display art during the Three Rivers Arts Festival each June.

TOP RIGHT: One Mellon Bank Center is a tribute to the Mellon family in Pittsburgh's business and philanthropic community.

RIGHT: Forbes Avenue downtown is a fine mix of restored period buildings, an inviting setting for lunchtime shoppers.

"*I don't really have an explanation for my fascination with the place, except perhaps that...Pittsburgh is where I became who I am now.*"

**Michael Chabon,
fiction writer**

LEFT: Besides summer activities on land and in the river, the Three Rivers Regatta features hot air ballooning from the Point. "Big Foot," a sneaker as tall as a ten-story building, inflates for launch.

ABOVE: The Smiley™ cookie, a symbol of Eat'n Park restaurants started by a Pittsburgher in 1949, prepares to soar safely beyond Mt. Washington while the grocery-laden bag of Shop n' Save, an area supermarket chain, entertains crowds at the Three Rivers Regatta.

ABOVE: Classic cars displayed on the mosaic granite plaza of PPG Place promote the Vintage Grand Prix, an annual car race run solely by volunteers as a charity to benefit autistic children.

TOP RIGHT: Viewed from the Liberty Bridge, a light rail transit system serves the downtown.

RIGHT: Building Gateway Center led Pittsburgh's post-World War II urban renewal that grabbed the attention of planners worldwide.

ABOVE: The futuristic gleam of One Oxford Centre's silver-painted glass and aluminum rise in contrast to the rugged granite of the Allegheny County Courthouse and Jail and the smooth front of the 1902 Frick Building.

TOP RIGHT: The north face of the Golden Triangle is striking from the neighborhood of Fineview.

RIGHT: Many of the vertical shafts along 4th Avenue near Wood Street reflect an era before skyscrapers and have been recycled through varying business uses.

ABOVE: Colorful lights at the tip of the Triangle and throughout the downtown render a brilliant evening skyline within the Three Rivers City.

RIGHT: This fountain stands in the park at Allegheny Courthouse.

LEFT: A glass dome decorates the terra cotta Rotunda, once a "turning place for taxis" at the Union Station. This Beaux Arts structure now leads to apartments rather than a railroad station.

TOP ABOVE: In the Terrace Room of the Westin William Penn Hotel, a mural by Andrew Karoly and Louis Szanto features British General Forbes and George Washington securing Fort Duquesne from the French.

ABOVE: History murals painted between 1938 and 1941 by nationally acclaimed Pittsburgh artist, Vincent Nesbert, hang in Allegheny County Courthouse.

FOLLOWING PAGES: Sunrise and night lights make this view from the West End Bridge spectacular.

ARTS ENSHRINED AND THE SCIENCES ADVANCED

There is no place like Pittsburgh for experiencing the public legacy contributed by wealthy entrepreneurs. Museums, parks, colleges, and halls bear their names, names such as Frick, Carnegie, Mellon, Heinz, Phipps, Scaife, Schenley, Hillman, and Benedum.

From each name unfolds a success story in which individuals reaped unprecedented profits, especially at the turn of the century, an era void of income tax and government regulations. Fashioning coke ovens to create a whole new industry, steel-making, produced millions for Henry Clay Frick, a financial and managerial wizard. The man who financed Frick's innovative plan, thus harnessing himself to a fortune-in-the-making, was banker Thomas Mellon. Henry J. Heinz, an enlightened employer, built a world wide food bottling company that emphasized quality manufacturing and powerful promotion. (Ads still offer a free Heinz pickle pin, a complimentary token of the company since the 1893 World's Fair.) With the acquisition of railroads and the American rights to the Bessemer process, Andrew Carnegie held the reigns of the U.S. steel industry by 1886. Steel was also the magnet that lured inventor George Westinghouse from New York to Pittsburgh, where he manufactured his inventions (361 received patents) that revolutionized railroading and electricity.

Andrew Carnegie devoted the latter part of his life to giving away more than $350 million. Fascinated with learning, in 1895 Carnegie established institutions such as the Carnegie Museums and Library that provided opportunities for self-education.

Spending time at the Carnegie—where I can enjoy literature, art, music, and science in one complex—is an irresistible opportunity for me as an out-of-towner.

Indoors, I first scaled the wide shallow steps of the Sarah Scaife Gallery of the Carnegie Museum of Art to gaze at works by such artists as Winslow Homer, Thomas Eakins, Henri Matisse, Georges Braque, and Anselm Kiefer. The Museum purchased their art over the past century before these creators were confirmed as masters by the art world. Selecting brilliant pieces from new talent has always been the role of the juried Carnegie International, North America's only large-scale survey of contemporary art. In another section of the Museum, the collections of the Heinz Architectural Center include the studio of master architect, Frank Lloyd Wright.

Moving to art of earlier periods in the Hall of Architecture, I was impressed by this exhibition of world-class casts, the largest in the United States.

In his endowments to his home city, Carnegie took pleasure in bringing to Pittsburgh what the majority could not go to see. At the founder's suggestion, paleontologists collected dinosaur bones and fossils from the American West as well as from around the world, gathering a remarkable collection for the Carnegie Museum of Natural History. It is awesome to gaze at the real skeleton of *Tyrannosaurus rex*, the largest land-roving carnivore ever to have lived.

The extensive subjects of the Museum's exhibits fascinate visitors. They revel in the beauty of the specimens in the Hillman Hall of Minerals & Gems, a Hillman Foundation gift inspired and supported by Pittsburgh businessman Henry Lea Hillman. In the Benedum Hall of Geology, a gift of the Claude Worthington Benedum Foundation, a ride in the Stratavator moves through 16,000 feet of rocks beneath Pittsburgh.

The Carnegie Lecture Hall is the long-time venue of the International Poetry Forum, a civic institution that has thrived in Pittsburgh's literary landscape since 1966. This midweek event brings out listeners to hear the likes of Russian poet Yevgeny Yevtushenko and actor Gregory Peck. Filling the house, Pittsburghers thrive on the pure art of poetry reading.

The cultural milieu that philanthropists influenced in Pittsburgh produced the prolific artist and trend setter who is now honored in the Andy Warhol Museum, a 1993 North Side addition to the Carnegie. Seven floors of galleries, the most comprehensive single-artist museum in the United States, show Andy Warhol's (1928-1987) art.

Nearby, another component of the Carnegie Museums of Pittsburgh, the Carnegie Science Center transforms the scientific world into wow! experiences with more than 250 interactive exhibits. If Carnegie could explore the Science Center's four floors of technological magic, he would be just as fascinated as visitors are today with its lasers, its robotics, and its historical miniature railroad display. Although the last would have been most familiar, the founder would have favored expanding the knowledge of ordinary citizens, including children.

Andrew Carnegie began working at the age of thirteen. His long days were enriched by the generosity of Colonel James Anderson, a neighbor who opened his home library to lads who had traded schooling for a paycheck. In appreciation, Andrew Carnegie endowed communities with public libraries, 2,800 worldwide.

With the Carnegie's eight acres a cultural linchpin of the East End, the neighborhood of Oakland is also home to the Carnegie Mellon University and the University of Pittsburgh, the former renowned for its frontline research in robotics and the latter in biomedicine. Pittsburgh spawned such breakthroughs as the Salk vaccine against polio and the identification of Vitamin C. Area research has made advances in cancer treatments.

One morning when Pitt students were on break, I toured three of the University's remarkable edifices in the central quadrangle. Designed by architect Charles Z. Klauder, they all have stained glass by Charles Connick and wrought iron by Samuel Yellin. These Gothic-style structures stand out on a 125-acre campus expanded from the initial fourteen acres donated by the Mellons.

I went first to the building everyone sees first, the Cathedral of Learning. From any vantage point in Oakland, this Gothic building with its graceful pinnacles unabashedly dominates the skyline. It is the tallest

classroom building in the Western World and the second tallest in the world, topped only by one in Moscow. During the Depression Pittsburgh schoolchildren contributed coins to support the Cathedral's construction. The Nationality Classrooms on the first and third floors are popular choices for professors and tourists.

On the main floor I marveled at one room transported from the country home of William Croghan, Jr. Although his sixteen-year-old daughter Mary eloped abroad with a forty-three-year-old Englishman, Captain Schenley in 1835, she did not forget her birthplace. Fifty-four years later, Mary Schenley's donation of 300 acres toward a city park helped Pittsburgh advance toward a new era of beautifying urban settings. Schenley Park in Oakland combines greenery with opportunities for leisure.

On Pitt's lawn to the east of the Cathedral, the Heinz Chapel, according to architectural historian Franklin Toker, "leaps up as a miniature mountain." In his will, Henry J. Heinz provided a bequest to the University to build a memorial in honor of his mother. After his death in 1919, his children added to the bequest and commissioned the Heinz Memorial Chapel. Construction began in 1933.

Today, this interfaith chapel is distinguished for its stained glass. The deeply hued windows in the transept, seventy-three feet high, reflect a rapturous glow in the late afternoon. The windows, with their 391 recognizable figures from history, were crafted by the Boston studio of Pittsburgh native Charles Connick.

The third Gothic structure that I went to was actually the first of the three to be dedicated. The Stephen Foster Memorial houses a museum, concert hall and research library dedicated to Stephen Collins Foster, the first professional songwriter. Composing truly down-home music in his Wood Street office, he sold such tunes as "Jeanie with the Light Brown Hair," "Oh! Susanna," and "Camptown Races" to minstrel groups. His lifetime (1826-1864) preceded sound recordings

"This city has a great tradition of founders—the founding of the first great Carnegie Library, the founding of corporations, hospitals, the founding of our History Center. . . . Pittsburgh is one of the most exciting cities in the world."

David McCullough, Pulitzer prizewinning historian

and fees for performing rights. He died poor although most Americans can hum at least a line from one of his 285 compositions.

The appeal of Foster's music inspired Josiah K. Lilly, the son of the founder of a pharmaceutical firm, to collect his songs and other memorabilia. These archives are now housed in the Stephen Foster Memorial, a structure built with small donations from the general public and a few larger ones from Lilly, A.W. Mellon and others. It was natural for the collections and the Memorial to be in Pittsburgh, the composer's birthplace.

Instead of building for the public, the Henry Clay Frick family donated their private property to the City of Pittsburgh. The 476-acre Frick Park welcomes rambling along its paths; a deep forest is also wheelchair-accessible. Within the Frick Art & Historical Center in the East End, Clayton, the family mansion, recreates the lavish Victorian lifestyle of an extremely wealthy family with young children. Among the nine thousand objects in the house are decorative arts held in high regard in the 1890s. Henry Clay's daughter, Helen Frick, who died in 1984 at the age of ninety-six, provided $6 million to restore and to maintain Clayton as it was during her childhood.

When Henry Phipps, a Carnegie manager, erected the Phipps Conservatory for the City in 1893, it was the largest Victorian glass house in the country. Within its nine rooms were exhibited many tropical plants that had been transported by rail from the Columbian Exposition in Chicago.

Today from its location in Schenley Park, the Conservatory's glass roofs beckon with an arabesque loftiness. Inside, in the Palm Court, I promptly felt drawn into lushness. In the Orchid Room, streaming sun and cascading water heightened my enjoyment of the exotic plants with blooms against mossy trunks. In past decades when industrial soot blanketed the city, the clean air within the Conservatory was an escape from Pittsburgh's pollution.

From its beginnings, Phipps intended that the Conservatory be "a source of instruction as well as pleasure to the people." Outdoors, I strolled through the Discovery Garden with exhibits stimulating to youngsters. Walking a bit farther, I enjoyed the artistic shapes of the bonsai—one of the largest collections in the country—in the Conservatory's Japanese Garden.

A strikingly different garden on the North Side's Sampsonia Way features sculpture that blends into the architectural history of a site where a building burned years ago. This multi-level garden by Philadelphia artist Winifred Lutz is within the collection of the Mattress Factory, one of the few museums in the world to commission installation art. In its enormous spaces, artists of international recognition construct art where it is exhibited, and some of

that art—for example, James Turrell's *Catso, Red, 1967*—remain in the Museum's permanent collection. Creating such a museum originated with Barbara Luderowski, whose determined vision includes new uses for other vacant buildings in the Federal-North district.

A short jaunt across the 6th Street Bridge leads to the stunning home of the Pittsburgh Symphony, Heinz Hall for the Performing Arts. In the late 1960's, the Howard Heinz Endowment committed to a $10 million restoration of this former plush movie house called Penn Theater. In 1982 a garden and addition financed by the Heinz philanthropies expanded the social areas surrounding the auditorium. In 1995, the Symphony's centennial year, improvements refined the concert hall's capability.

Supported in part by the Heinz Endowments since its inception in 1984, the Pittsburgh Cultural Trust

developed a long-range design for the Penn-Liberty area of the Downtown to be a concentration of arts and entertainment venues. Besides the restoration of Heinz Hall, plans for the fourteen-block Cultural District encompassed the construction of the Theater Square project at 7th Street and Penn Avenue and the resurrection of two theaters.

For one, the former Stanley Theater, the Claude Worthington Benedum Foundation provided a grant toward a $42 million restoration. The Benedum Center now hosts the Pittsburgh Opera, the Ballet Theater, the Civic Light Opera, the Pittsburgh Dance Council, and the Broadway series, which is shared with Heinz Hall and the Byham. A former vaudeville house, the Byham is now an intimate theater named to honor William C. and Carolyn M. Byham, a Pittsburgh couple who with Heinz Endowments and the Commonwealth of Pennsylvania, donated renovation funds.

Private monies and government funds have created a Cultural District brimming with art and energy. Annual performances in the Cultural District of the Golden Triangle soared after one decade.

What wealthy entrepreneurs contributed to the arts and sciences during Pittsburgh's industrial heyday is now enshrined in structures managed by institutions that still educate and delight. What philanthropic citizens support now presents Pittsburgh as a model for cooperation between government, foundations, and businesses throughout the country and the world. Inspired by a rich, cultural legacy, the people of Pittsburgh thrive on the disciplines of art and science.

PAGE 55: Resembling the interior of the Parthenon, the Carnegie's Hall of Sculpture exhibits classical masterpieces and accommodates art classes and other events.

PAGE 57: Andy Warhol's portrait of Andrew Carnegie hangs in the Carnegie Museum of Art.

ABOVE: As Founder Andrew Carnegie wished, other benefactors supported arts for the public. Since opening in 1974, the Sarah Scaife Gallery expanded the

permanent collection of the Carnegie
Museum of Art. Later, the Heinz
Galleries for Changing Exhibits and
the Ailsa Mellon Bruce Galleries for the
Decorative Arts also opened.

RIGHT: Architectural casts of the
twelfth century portals of the French
Abbey of St. Gilles are among other
antiquities in the Art Museum's Hall
of Architecture.

ABOVE: The underground realities of Pennsylvania, including the rich deposits of coal, oil, and natural gas, tell Pittsburgh's story in the Benedum Hall of Geology within the Carnegie Museum of Natural History.

RIGHT: Since 1907 people have come to the Carnegie, "the home of the dinosaurs," to view the skeletons of these ancient but extinct animals up close. Many of these dinosaurs were collected over 14 years of difficult work in the Utah desert that is now Dinosaur National Park.

LEFT: Ticketholders to such events as poetry readings by the International Poetry Forum socialize in the ornate foyer of the Carnegie Music Hall.

ABOVE: The Library of the Stephen Foster Memorial on the University of Pittsburgh campus contains first-edition reproductions of Foster's music, a roller organ, a Regina music box, an early disc phonograph, and Thomas Hicks' 1852 oil portrait of Stephen Foster, the first professional songwriter in the United States.

NEXT PAGES: "Cows," a work of art by Andy Warhol, hangs in a seven-floor museum that is devoted solely to the artist. The Andy Warhol Museum is a North Side component of the Carnegie Museums and Library.

"This city felt like home from the first day we arrived."

Salvadore Silipigni, cellist, Pittsburgh Symphony Orchestra

TOP LEFT: Graduates of institutions seeded by wealthy donors have spawned high-tech research companies in Pittsburgh. Red Zone Robotics, a firm located in Lawrenceville in the very brick building where George Westinghouse launched his air brake manufacturing, designed and assembled Rosie, a robot that can operate tools in hazardous environments such as nuclear power plants.

LEFT: A young Pittsburgher observes his portrait which will be drawn by a robot in the Carnegie Science Center located on the North Side.

ABOVE: The rotunda of an historic post office captures the imaginations of youngsters who visit the site, now the Pittsburgh Children's Museum.

ABOVE: Designed as a community center with a gymnasium, swimming pool and library, the Carnegie Library of Homestead was given to this town of steelworkers by Andrew Carnegie.

RIGHT: Young dancers practice at the dance studio of the Civic Light Opera, which performs in the restored Benedum Center for the Performing Arts on Penn Avenue.

LEFT: During the Depression years, at ten cents per brick, Pittsburghers contributed to the building of the Cathedral of Learning, the tallest classroom building in the Western Hemisphere. Its Gothic features make the Commons Room on the main floor notable.

ABOVE: The Cathedral of Learning (center) stands out in an aerial of Oakland, home of several educational institutions including Carnegie Mellon University and University of Pittsburgh. To the east (top of photo) stretch adjoining residential neighborhoods of Shadyside and Squirrel Hill.

ABOVE: As a top research center, the University of Pittsburgh attracts approximately 30,000 students from many countries and ethnic backgrounds to its Oakland campus.

RIGHT: Within the Cathedral of Learning the Syria-Lebanon Room is one of twenty-odd Nationality Classrooms, each a gift to the University of Pitt from an ethnic group of Allegheny County. One of the few not used for classes, this room is a library of a nomad.

NEXT PAGES: Bronze and crystal chandeliers and a Venetian baroque ceiling accent the grandeur of Heinz Hall, home of the Pittsburgh Symphony.

LEFT: This chandelier embellishes the auditorium of the Benedum Center for Performing Arts, which is used by several dance and drama groups.

ABOVE: Built in 1858, the Allegheny Observatory on a North Side hilltop, boasts the fourth largest photographic refracting telescope in the world.

TOP ABOVE: The stained glass windows of Heinz Memorial Chapel depict 391 identifiable people throughout history. The Truth window on the south wall includes Sir Isaac Newton and Emily Dickinson.

ABOVE: Dorothea Dix, American social reformer who pressed for improvements in prisons and asylums, is in the Chapel's Tolerance window, north wall.

RIGHT: Wealthy donors often built churches. The Mellons constructed the Gothic-style East Liberty Presbyterian Church in that neighborhood.

ABOVE: At Clayton, the Victorian mansion where Adelaide and Henry Clay Frick raised their family, visitors can observe the lifestyle of one of the wealthiest young couples in nineteenth century America.

TOP RIGHT: The Carriage Museum at the Frick Art & Historical Center dis-plays transportation means at the dawn of the automotive age.

RIGHT: Mahogany furniture (1892) and a Bouveret painting enrich the Frick family dining room at Clayton, a house museum within the Frick Art & Historical Center.

"Poetry readings in Pittsburgh are "not such a big deal." We have become habituated to them as the seasons of the year or our skylines."

**Samuel Hazo
founder,
International
Poetry Forum**

ABOVE: Garden displays in the Victorian glasshouse of the Phipps Conservatory draw visitors to this attraction in the city's Schenley Park.

RIGHT: The beauty of the Conservatory's annual Fall Flower Show reflects the desire of its donor, steel magnate Henry Phipps, to bring "pleasure to the people."

A CITY OF FAMILY NEIGHBORHOODS

For years Mister Fred Rogers has told millions of children around the world that it is a beautiful day in his neighborhood. That that neighborhood is Pittsburgh may come as a surprise to many of his "television neighbors." The field trips to the planetarium, a recycling plant, or a dance theatre introduce young children to a Pittsburgh sampling of neighborhood resources. And grown children remember that in Mister Rogers' Neighborhood, people felt safe and special.

Pittsburgh has more than its share of neighborliness. People reach out. A ten-year resident who stayed after college called it "a most inviting town." Some would protest their cosmopolitan city being dubbed a town, but Pittsburgh extends a Midwestern casualness. Its people are approachable; its pace less frenetic than that of other major cities. One native on her way back for graduate studies anticipated returning because "its social fabric seems more flexible than Boston's crust, for example; but there are intellectual and artistic opportunities equal to those in D.C."

Pittsburgh's closely knit neighborhoods figured positively in its 1985 rating by the Places Rated Almanac as the most livable city in America. The tribute acknowledges that diversity and ethnicity run deep into the cultural bedrock of Pittsburgh. The way people eat, worship, and celebrate affirms ethnic ties. According to one seasoned observer, the great grandchildren of the original immigrants are carrying the torch of their heritage—and proudly.

But while Pittsburghers claim their own past and its distinctions, they are multicultural in spirit. For example, although Etna has been an Italian enclave, residents from other backgrounds are comfortable in this community north of the City. Most Pittsburghers would understand the young person who commented, "I'm Polish and German, but I like Italian food the best."

I headed to the Senator John Heinz Pittsburgh Regional History Center in the Strip District to enjoy an overview of the ethnic smorgasbord Pittsburghers

"Pittsburgh's greatest asset is the warmth and character of its people."

Kevin McClatchy, CEO, Pittsburgh Pirates

owned long before it was fashionable. Throughout this seven-floor building–once a warehouse for an ice company–are emblazoned stories of Western Pennsylvanians who networked their way across from Europe and up from the South over the past 250 years. Family connections drew immigrants from *paesi* (villages) in Italy to settlements here such as Bloomfield. Germans settled near each other in Spring Hill, and Eastern European steel and rail workers rapidly nestled into the flats and then the slopes of the South Side.

The History Center focuses on stories about these and other Western Pennsylvanians who contributed to the industrial success of the region. The videos, photos and artifacts on display confirm a vivid tie between the region's past and present. During the campaign to fund the History Center, Honorary Chair David McCullough, a native who hosted Public Broadcasting Service's "American Experience," aptly described this reality when he wrote: "There is no such thing as the past, there is only somebody else's present."

The exhibit of Lilian Carter's bass and George Benson's electric guitar arranged in a club setting reminded me of how jazz rhythms have vibrated out of the Hill District ever since musicians like Lena Horne stopped here to jam on cross-country trips. There are hands-on opportunities for children to learn about their past. When children pack plastic pickles in jars in Discovery Place, they grasp a bit of the working day of youths who worked for the Heinz Company. They can also "Climb in a Steel Mill."

In this Center, which also houses the region's largest collection of printed and archival materials about the counties in Western Pennsylvania, history butts up against the present. While sitting in the restored Streetcar 1724 on exhibit on the first floor, a Pittsburgh native remembered that "the red ones were the nicest to ride, especially to Kennywood." A display on another floor depicts Italian greengrocers who hawked their produce before Asian vendors and landmark restaurants populated the Strip.

Today the District's well-known eateries sell such legends as broccoli bread, chocolate cake to die for, a late-night sandwich stuffed with french fries, and seafood fresher than one can imagine. Old timers treasure memories from a time when the Strip swarmed with just as much business but fewer vehicles. One Mt. Washington retiree recalls his mother holding his hand and balancing a basket of tomatoes on her head on the walk from market across the Smithfield Bridge, climbing home up to Sycamore Street.

In every pocket of Pittsburgh, there are layers of ethnicity. The History Center invites residents to donate objects and stories, adding their own family's chapter to the collective history of the Region.

Over the past two centuries nationality transitions occurred in all areas. For example, Lawrenceville, an East End neighborhood sandwiched between the Allegheny River and rail lines, was settled in the early decades of the

1800s by English and Scots-Irish such as songwriter Stephen Foster's father. Irish and German Catholics replaced them in the mid-nineteenth century; and, by the turn of the next one, Polish laborers settled close to the heavy industries that had begun to flex their muscles.

Although the majority of residents in the West End's Chartiers are African Americans, with many of German descent populating Troy Hill on the North Side, residents of varied nationalities blend in neighborhoods. A sixty-year-old life resident explained that ethnicity does not align with streets as it often did in the 1940s, "My children married every shade, and ethnic background is hardly a factor in where they live."

After World War II, third-generation Pittsburghers wrestled with their ethnic traditions, aspiring to live the American dream in the suburbs. However, more recent attitudes have brought restoration and conversion to

hillside rowhouses and abandoned warehouses. For example, professionals are transforming the storefronts on the eastern end of Butler Street into offices, and high-tech firms are filling former manufacturing plants with industrial design workspace.

Today the City markets its ninety neighborhoods as welcome real estate opportunities. A non-profit organization steers potential city-dwellers to data useful in selecting a community. Street signs also identify neighborhoods, and Pittsburghers consider their city richly diverse rather than parochial.

In 1925 Chancellor John G. Bowman of the University of Pittsburgh solicited immigrant residents to construct classrooms "that would reflect their cultural heritage from the Old World." Each of the Nationality Classrooms in the Cathedral of Learning depicts a country in a specific time frame prior to 1787 when the University was founded. Each room–filled with symbolic features and artifacts–was planned and sponsored by a local committee under the guidance of Sociology Professor Ruth Crawford Mitchell. As a result, Pittsburgh workers aspired to send their children to Pitt, and scholarship money is still linked with each classroom. A tour of the twenty-some Nationality Classrooms reveals many cultural symbols representing the heritage of countries as varied as Israel, Russia, and France.

In addition to touring, I enjoyed *experiencing* culture at some of the area's public ethnic events. They are numerous. For instance, at Kennywood in summer there are at least ten ethnic days such as Hungarian Day, and the Gateway Clipper riverboat offers cruises–for example, Spanish Night or Slovenian Night–that celebrate nationalities from around the world.

Occasionally, Duquesne University's Tamburitzans, an internationally famous dance troupe, perform in their city of origin. Since 1937, these scholarship recipients keep alive the music and dances of folk cultures.

In March the St. Patrick's Day Parade takes green and hoopla to the Downtown, and in October the City spares no fanfare for Columbus Day.

In May at St. Nicholas Cathedral in Oakland thousands of Pittsburghers relish the traditional specialties served at this Greek Food Festival. This parish prepares Greek recipes from scratch. Volunteers turn 1,700 pounds of ground meat into 10,250 *souzoukakia*, meatballs in wine sauce. Piecework assignments are based on skills honored over the years. Certain workers curl the diples; others layer the *pastitsio* or cut up ingredients for the cooks. The result is a superb homecooked cuisine.

Anticipation mounts as young dancers in black vests slip past the queue of hungry people and head toward the stage. Beyond the food lines, live *bouzouki* music from various islands floats across a sea of round tables. In this great room, bright with halogen lights, the Greek wall posters look miniature, but the piles of pastries assure me that there will be plenty of *finikia* and diples. The walnut-filled *karithopeta* is as rich as it is dark, and the layers of pastry in the *baklava* are tissue-thin. No wonder the bakers annually make more than 10,000 servings of this famous Greek dessert.

Faces relax as people socialize in this festive setting. One couple converses in Greek; at least seventy percent of the Cathedral's 600 families speak the tongue of the motherland. Classes in Greek language and traditional dances share culture with the next generation.

Because Pittsburgh generational ties are so strong, it is not uncommon for young professionals to return to the city of their birth when they begin to rear a family. When grandparents live within walking distance, it is all in a week's happenings for three generations to spend time together.

On a steamy July evening, a three-generation family was awaiting the parade that would launch South Side Summer Street Spectacular festival. As her grandchildren licked ice balls, the grandmother summed up her Pittsburgh roots in the South Side flats. "I live on Sarah Street in the same house where I was born and raised eight children." Sarah, Mary, Jane, and Sidney are among the streets named after family members of John Ormsby, a British major who in 1752 settled on the flatland between the Monongahela River and the slopes of Mt. Washington. Known as Birmingham, this area thrived industrially with sixty-eight glass factories producing half of the nation's glass supply by 1870. In the twentieth century her husband settled here to work on the railroads, and her children played in the same community where she had grown. "I remember coming to parades along this street when I was little," this grandmother recounted.

On any day of the year the flavor of the South Side feels real over an Iron City and a thick kielbassi sandwich at any number of watering holes along Carson Street. However, on Saturday at the Festival's Perfect Pierogie Cookoff, judges chose the best cook of this Polish specialty. A pierogie is a noodle dough dumpling filled traditionally with potatoes, prunes, or fried cabbage. On that day pierogies, fresh and frozen, disappeared for the benefit of a South Side hospital. According to one observer, "A lot of Irish people were eating them too."

Authentic foods, music, and dances characterize the Pittsburgh Folk Festival, an annual weekend celebrating the heritage of many nationalities. I bought homemade delicacies from people who knew how they were made—nut horns or kifflies at the Hungarian booth and cheese crepes from a member of the choir of the Holy Trinity Serbian Orthodox Cathedral. For generations, churches have perpetuated ethnic allegiance, but as small neighborhood churches and parochial schools close, Pittsburghers enthusiastically attend events such as the Festival to sample a wide array of cuisines and to buy heirloom crafts.

Tens of thousands also gather for the Pittsburgh Vintage Grand Prix, a classic car rally and race on a tortuous 2.3 mile route in the City's Schenley Park. Run totally by volunteers, thousands of them, the week-long event illustrates Pittsburgh's generosity, in this case for the families of autistic children.

Besides the citywide generosity that shines in behalf of worthwhile causes such as the Autism Society of Pittsburgh, many individuals exert effort to improve their neighborhoods, irrespective of the ethnic mix. One City employee enjoys the rewards of organizing a scholarship fund for instrumental students in his neighborhood school. Dozens of retirees tutor and counsel at community centers. Neighbors plant corner gardens to brighten their streets. For Pittsburghers, it *is* a beautiful day in their neighborhood.

PAGE 86 AND LEFT: Neighborhood parades, such as this kickoff for a festival on the South Side, thrill Pittsburgh communities.

ABOVE: At the South Side Summer Street Spectacular, the city's largest neighborhood festival, residents express their fun-loving spirit along Carson Street.

PREVIOUS PAGES: One of the street names harking back to its Bavarian origins, Woesner Avenue follows a steep grade in Spring Hill.

ABOVE: West North Avenue is one of the North Side's historic Mexican War Streets. Their name originated with General William Robinson, Jr., who in 1848 planned this section of what was then Allegheny City and named the new streets after the generals and battles of the Mexican War from which he had just returned.

RIGHT: The center dwelling, the 1870s Reineman House, shares meticulous preservation with other architecturally interesting homes in Pittsburgh neighborhoods. The historic House stands on Lowrie Street in Troy Hill, a once-German neighborhood on a steep slope high above the Allegheny River.

LEFT: The skyline from Spring Hill, one of the City's ninety neighborhoods, accentuates the essence of Pittsburgh architecture—variety.

ABOVE: Shops serve residents of Shadyside, the heart of Pittsburgh's fashionable East End situated four miles east of Downtown.

NEXT PAGES: From Federal Street on the north shore of the Allegheny River, the downtown skyline, including (l to r) Gulf Tower, USX Tower, One Mellon Bank Center, One PNC Plaza, and CNG Tower, dominates the horizon.

ABOVE: Internationally known bassist Dwayne Dolphin poses near a mural of jazz greats by Pittsburgher Walt Sims, Jr. at Dizzy's, a jazz and blues restaurant in the Strip District.

RIGHT: Internationally acclaimed Tamburitzans, a forty-member student troupe of folk dancers and musicians from Duquesne University, perform tours around the country.

*"Pittsburgh was
my first American
home. It is still as
important to me as
ever. I would love
to see it become a
'model city' with
the private and
public sectors,
foundations, and
government working
together on
tough issues."*

**Teresa Heinz, Heinz
Family Foundation**

LEFT: A mural by Judy Penzer on a Penn Avenue building brightens the neighborhood of Friendship.

ABOVE: Youthful dancers entertain diners at the Greek Food Festival, an annual event at the St. Nicholas Greek Orthodox Cathedral.

ABOVE: Lebanese dancers perform at the Pittsburgh Folk Festival, a smorgasboard of ethnic foods, crafts and shows.
RIGHT: To experience an authentic German beer hall, Pittsburghers go to the North Side's Penn Brewery owned by Tom Pastorius, a direct descendent of the founder of the first German settlement in America. This micro-brewery and restaurant are housed in restored buildings of the Eberhardt & Ober Brewery in a hilltop neighborhood with a village ambience.
NEXT PAGES: The skyline with St. John the Baptist Ukrainian Catholic Church, South Side, symbolizes a blend of the past with the present in Pittsburgh.

ABOVE: The Senator John Heinz Pittsburgh Regional History Center displays the sanctuary of the Orthodox Synagogue, Machsikei Hadas, once on Wylie Avenue in the Hill District.

RIGHT: Among Pittsburgh's many houses of worship is the Rodef Shalom Temple at 5th and Morewood Avenues in Oakland.

LEFT: A visitor to the Senator John Heinz Pittsburgh Regional History Center peers into the kitchen of a reconstructed 1950s suburban tract house, one of three dwellings in the permanent exhibit, "Points in Time: Building a Life in Western PA, 1750-Today."

ABOVE: In a History Center exhibit illustrating that the first car hop originated in Pittsburgh, a 1956 Chevrolet Bel Air Sports Coupe pulls up to a popular eatery's neon sign, designed in 1959.

FOLLOWING PAGES: The Ukrainian Classroom in the Cathedral of Learning at the University of Pittsburgh features furnishings and decorative arts from the Ukraine.

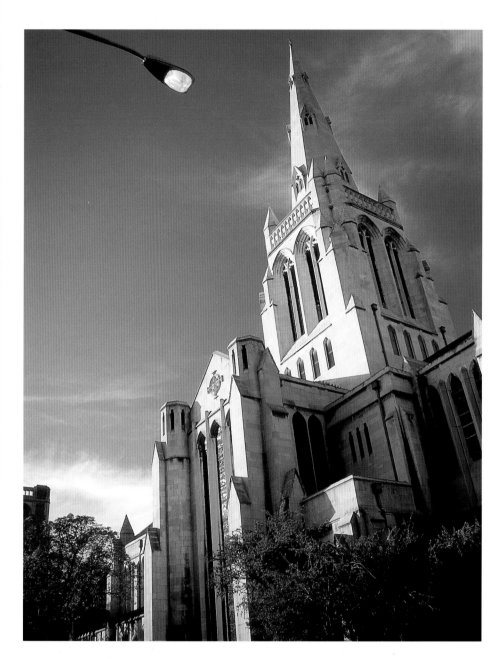

LEFT: In St. Nicholas Greek Orthodox Cathedral in Oakland, according to Byzantine arrangement, an icon screen separates the sanctuary from the nave. During Greek Festival tours visitors learn that among the many icons and images, the peacocks on the Royal Doors stand for eternity.

ABOVE: Within the tranquil, landscaped residential neighborhood of Shadyside are prominent churches such as Cavalry Epispocal Church.

ABOVE RIGHT: Detail, door, St Paul's Cathedral, Oakland, a church moved from downtown at the turn of the twentieth century.

IN PITTSBURGH AND BEYOND

In this inland city there are many attractions with an international flair. Such architectural jewels as the Heinz Chapel and Station Square One Building create a sense of Renaissance Europe, and the classical design of the Mellon Institute evokes ancient Greece. Exhibits at Pittsburgh's museums, for example, the Carnegie, have a world-wide reach. During one of my visits to the City, even the realities of Antarctica came alive at an exhibit at the Carnegie Science Museum.

On another occasion my memories of East Africa returned. At the Pittsburgh Zoo we had climbed uphill through the Asian Forest and then wound around a grassy bend towards the African Savanna, where a giraffe was twirling a leaf with her fourteen-inch tongue. The sight of elephants rolling in the mud and stuffing their mouths with their trunks reminded me of gamepark runs in Kenya. As in the wild, weaver birds rode on the elephants' gray backs to catch insects, and zebras grazed in the background. The Zoo's Savanna even smelled like the pungent grasslands of Masai Mara. I wanted to tell every little kid who was pointing, "Yes, look, because this is exactly the way these mammals behave in the wilds in Africa!"

The Zoo's other 4,000 animals also enjoy carefully designed natural environments. In the Tropical Forest, a simulation of the habitat that supports more than half of the world's plant and animal species, colorful mandrills from West Africa move continually on all fours while white-cheeked gibbons travel hand-over-hand between limbs in the lush greenery. In the AquaZoo at least a dozen penguins enjoy friendship in a chilly community setting.

Kids Kingdom, "where kids play like the animals," is a particularly popular section of the Zoo. Within the interactive exhibits, young visitors can cross a bridge suspended high in the tree canopy, slide like penguins, and crawl underground to gaze face to face with meerkats, those inquisitive members of the mongoose family.

The National Aviary in Pittsburgh offers firsthand encounters with exotic birds. Upon my arrival at this North Side attraction, Archie, a hyacinth macaw and long-time resident, squawked an unforgettable greeting.

I followed a staffer's recommendation and sat down to observe in the Bridge Room. Within minutes, birds of varying sizes accepted my presence and continued preening, eating, and socializing. I appreciated the beauty of the Blue Crowned Pigeon, the largest pigeon in the world. The antics of some species were amusing–the bobbing head of the Coral billed Ground Cuckoo and the beak action of Jackson's Hornbill, for example.

Enjoying an aviary is not a quick-cut experience digested with a few soundbites and keyboard punches. In the Marsh Room, created by a grant from the Mary Scaife Foundation, Greater Flamingos, Scarlet Ibises, and Roseate Spoonbills strutted and soared. Other birds, resplendent with afternoon light, filtered water through their beaks in search of tasty tidbits. Two hundred bird species feel at home in this climate-controlled Aviary.

The Aviary was granted national designation by the United States Congress in 1993, a result of Pittsburghers' determined drive to have in their city an institution with a profile comparable to the National Zoo in Washington D.C. and the National Aquarium in Baltimore.

This spirit has been evident in Western Pennsylvania since the first settlers headed west across the ridges. Within and beyond the Three Rivers City, people have planted ideas that have left meaningful legacies. Inventiveness and pluck spurred developments that pushed America toward her zenith. John Augustus Roebling fashioned wire rope essential for the building of suspension spans such as the Brooklyn Bridge. Also in the mid-nineteenth century, industrialist Samuel Kier was among the first to recognize the potential value of the petroleum seeping into his salt mines and marketed it both locally and as far as Europe. Charles M. Hall, whose process turns bauxite into aluminum, established the aluminum industry with the support of Pittsburgh investors. In the 1990s Linda Froehlich's spring and form company spent years acquiring a patent for the Super Clip, a clip that doesn't tear papers and is too all-around good to throw away.

In the arts and sciences, Pittsburghers demonstrate

remarkable prowess and energy. In medicine, Dr. Thomas Starzl pioneered liver transplantation, developing a drug to prevent organ rejection. Ceramist William Strickland, a 1996 McArthur "genius" Award winner, founded the Bidwell/Manchester Craftsmen's Guild to train at-risk youth in an income-generating program. Award-winning playwright August Wilson universalizes his Pittsburgh experience in insightful pieces of drama such as "Jitney" and "Fences."

In 1903 with teams of horses moving the earth, Henry C. Fownes built Oakmont, a national historic landmark golf course acclaimed in its original design by professionals. In at least two other instances locals have

first to wear numbers so that fans could identify the players. Today, the Steelers receive almost rabid support from their fans, who keep alive the tradition of swinging the "Terrible Towel" to emphasize their allegiance.

I headed past Three Rivers, the Steelers' home stadium, and traveled north on Route 28, passing the worker towns of Millvale, Etna and Aspinwall. At the next town's exit, I wound through the streets of Springdale, a town with a power plant and a coal mine, and up Colfax Hill to the childhood home of Rachel Carson, the scientist who alerted the world to the life-threatening dangers of pesticides.

No wonder Carson's appreciation of nature grew

originated ideas that produce fun. George Ferris invented the ferris wheel, an amusement park ride used across the globe. For three generations, the Zambelli Family has designed fireworks to thrill crowds around the country.

Teamwork is part of the spirit in Western Pennsylvania. The nation's first radio station, KDKA, and the country's first public television station, WQED, resulted from the cooperation of community trailblazers.

Team spirit also marks Pittsburgh sports. The City's major professional teams—the Penguins in ice hockey, the Pirates in baseball and the Steelers in football—have earned the loyalty of devoted fans who cheer that spirit. Way back in 1908, Pittsburgh's football team was the

throughout her years on this verdant hillside. Large hemlocks shelter a springhouse built by Carson's father. Although their home lacked plumbing and electricity, the Carson family entertained themselves with piano music and books..

Carson studiously moved through high school and college. As a researcher, she methodically recorded her observations, the genesis of her belief in the interdependence of all of life. In her final book, *Silent Spring* (1962), she gave a clarion call for humans to share responsibility for the survival of the planet. Even as cancer drained her strength, she spoke publicly of the detriment of pesticides to all living things.

Today schoolchildren visit the Rachel Carson Homestead to experience the wonder of nature and to grasp how the thorough research of this caring woman resulted in the banning of the chemical DDT in America. Education about the dangers of other pesticides continues in Carson's girlhood home.

Twenty minutes east in Fox Chapel, groups of children and adults also enjoy educational programs at Beechwood Farms Nature Reserve, a combined venture of the Audubon Society of Western Pennsylvania and the Western Pennsylvania Conservancy. Within the Reserve's 134 acres, several habitats demonstrate how ecosystems work. Beside a pond where Canada geese parent their fuzzy goslings, a mother and her son watched a redwing woo a mate. Some children traced food chains while volunteers repotted native seedlings. In the Discovery Room, a bright indoor area for exploring elements of nature, a huge black snake uncoiled against the glass.

I tend to think of Conservancy projects as wild, untouched acreage. In reality, this organization sets aside environments for public enjoyment. The Conservancy recycles prime lands by buying and sell-ing them at cost to public agencies for parks, forests, and gamelands. Since 1932, the Conservancy has been dogged in realizing its mission, protecting nearly 200,000 acres of wild beauty in Western Pennsylvania.

Beechwood is one of more than seventy-five Conservancy land acquisitions. Another that has become one of the best whitewater recreational areas in the East is a fourteen-mile stretch of the Youghiogheny River Gorge within Ohiopyle State Park. The beauty of this Park's ravines woos many Pennsylvanians to Fayette County where some visitors tour Kentuck Knob, a residence of fieldstone and red cypress designed by the eminent architect Frank Lloyd Wright.

The Conservancy also oversees Wright's world-renowned Fallingwater built in 1936 as a weekend retreat for the Edgar Kaufmann family. Over a cascading stream, Wright dramatically balanced several living levels made of sandstone quarried from the property. Rocks and water embrace the building voted in 1991 by the American Institute of Architects as "the best all-time work of American architecture." One critic has deemed the structure "Wright's greatest

essay in horizontal space."

Surrounding Fallingwater stretch 5,000 acres known as Bear Run Nature Reserve. One Pittsburgher who enjoys its marked trails today recalls the creekside cottage her family gave up when the Conservancy bought the land as a public trust in 1963.

For generations, area residents have headed to Kennywood, an amusement park that opened in 1898 on a shady country site frequented by picnickers. To entice Pittsburghers to ride the trolley on weekends, the Monongahela Street Railway Company created a trolley park and offered rides, games, concerts, and a lake for boating as well as a picnic grove. People from throughout the steel-making Monongahela Valley responded in droves, largely because the Park was marketed for groups–school groups in the spring, church and company picnics and ethnic festivals in the summer.

As a result, virtually every lifetime Pittsburgher holds a Kennywood memory bank. Great grandparents recall movie flip cards and the swan ride, grandmothers remember riding No. 68 trolley to Kennywood, and parents are delighted that the Log Jammer and corn dogs are just like they used to be. In honor of its multi-generational impact, Kennywood is one of two amusement parks designated as a National Historic Landmark.

Over the years Kennywood expanded its attractions, flexibly responding to the attraction thrills of each decade. Still open, however, is the Park's famous landmark, the orange Noah's Ark, a rocking walk-thru. But on hand are attractions that spark contemporary thrills. For example, two geysers operated by an employee soak riders of the Raging Rapids.

But as rides in a traditional amusement park, Kennywood's roller coasters win any bet. King of all the old-style wooden ones is the Thunderbolt; near the end of its 3,300 feet of track, the train drops an unthinkable 90 feet. The Jack Rabbit, a train that plunges a seventy-foot double dip into a natural ravine, also offers those bone-wrenching jerks that are absent in a ride on steel such as the Steel Phantom, the Park's

> *"Pittsburgh has a dynamic quality that few other places have. It has a past of historic importance to America and a world future that is unlimited."*
>
> **John E. Connelly, owner, Gateway Clipper Fleet**

and the world's fastest looping coaster.

To ride Kennywood's Merry-Go-Round is to enjoy a well-maintained and favorite antique. Ever since 1926, four rows of horses gallop to the music of a Wurlitzer Band Organ with 1,500 lights aglow.

Nightclub music by top-name performers is only one of the draws to Pittsburgh's Sandcastle, an entertainment complex on the "Mon" created by Kennywood's owners. With vision, they turned the abandoned railyard of a Homestead steel mill into a landscaped riverfront site with an old-fashioned boardwalk, plunging waterslides, sand volleyball courts, and race car tracks.

Among the numerous sites in Western Pennsylvania that celebrate its history are Fort Ligonier and Old Economy Village. Fort Ligonier is a reconstruction of the 1758-1766 original that figured heavily in the efforts of the English and Americans to secure the area against the French and their Native American allies. Located along America's transcontinental Route 30, Fort Ligonier bids visitors to experience living history events and to tour a spacious museum.

Old Economy Village in Ambridge is another type of museum, in this case a restoration of buildings depicting the lifestyle of an early nineteenth century religious community. George Rapp's Harmonist Society crossed the Atlantic and the Alleghenies and then settled in Beaver County to purify themselves for Christ's return. The buildings where they lived reflect their industriousness, and their love of art, gardens, and learning with no private ownership or child-rearing.

The pioneering spirit with which the Harmonists organized industries and their households reflects the human strength undergirding communities of the Pittsburgh area. With a profound sense of their history–immigrants and pioneers enduring while crossing both cultural and physical chasms–Western Pennsylvanians exercise their creativity with perseverance, support community endeavors with ardor and enjoy life with neighborly friendliness.

PAGE 115: Rafters enjoy rapids on the Youghiogheny River.

PAGE 116: At Sandcastle, an entertainment complex along "the Mon," there are thrilling waterslides, a riverfront boardwalk, and big-name concerts.

ABOVE: The New Guinea Crowned Pigeon poses at the National Aviary in Pittsburgh's North Side.

TOP RIGHT: Winter brings snow for such sports as downhill and cross-country skiing in the Laurel Highlands southeast of Pittsburgh.

RIGHT: At the Pittsburgh Zoo, elephants live in a natural habitat.

ABOVE: The Pittsburgh Steelers, multiple Super Bowl champions, play football at home in Three Rivers Stadium.

RIGHT: Loyal fans of the Pirates, Pittsburgh's professional baseball team, collect memorabilia from their long, colorful history in the Three Rivers City.

"It's the people that matter most, the people in the organization, the fans, and it will always be that way in Pittsburgh."

**Dan Rooney,
president,
Pittsburgh Steelers**

TOP LEFT: Celebrations such as weddings and festivals take place on Gateway Clipper riverboats on Pittsburgh's three rivers.

LEFT: Excursions on the Majestic or other vessels of the Gateway Clipper fleet delight visitors and locals.

ABOVE: Started as a picnic park along a trolley line, Kennywood thrills roller coaster aficionados with such rides as the Steel Phantom. "Lost Kennywood" recalls the Luna Park, an amusement park set up to showcase electric lighting.

TOP LEFT: At the Pennsylvania Trolley Museum in Washington, a trainman welcomes visitors aboard for a trolley ride. The museum has forty-two trolleys.

FAR LEFT: In the Allegheny Cemetery rest such celebrities as actress Lillian Russell, songwriter Stephen Foster, and performer Don Brockett.

LEFT: Despite their wilderness surroundings in 1824, the Harmonists enjoyed art and music at their religious community in Ambridge, Old Economy Village.

ABOVE: Once the summer home of Pittsburgh department store owner, E. J. Kaufmann, Fallingwater was designed by architect Frank Lloyd Wright.

ABOVE: More than 10,000 runners participate in Race For The Cure, a five-kilometer race/walk for breast cancer in Schenley Park in May.

RIGHT: The Pittsburgh Penguins, Stanley Cup holders, play ice hockey in Pittsburgh's Civic Arena.

READING SOURCES

Alberts, Robert C. **The Shaping of the Point: Pittsburgh's Renaissance Park**. Pittsburgh: University of Pittsburgh Press, 1980. A well-chronicled account of designing Pittsburgh's Point, a valuable part of Renaissance I.

Evert, Marilyn **Discovering Pittsburgh's Sculpture**. Pittsburgh: University of Pittsburgh Press, 1983. Illustrated description of Pittsburgh's pieces of sculpture and biographies of their sculptors.

Kidney, Walter C. **Landmark Architecture: Pittsburgh and Allegheny County**. Pittsburgh: Pittsburgh History & Landmarks Foundation, 1985. Descriptions with locations and photographs of individual structures follow chronological text about architectural styles in the region.

Lorant, Stefan **Pittsburgh: The Story of An American City**. Lenox, MA: Authors Edition, Inc., 1975. Detailed presentation of the city's history and culture, including personalities, up to the date of publication, incl. b&w photos.

Sajna, Mike **The Allegheny River: Watershed of the Nation.** University Park: The Pennsylvania State University Press, 1992. Color photos by Jim Schafer. Valuable account of one of Pittsburgh's three rivers.

Smith, Arthur G. **Pittsburgh Then and Now.** Pittsburgh: University of Pittsburgh Press, 1990. B&w photo spreads show a city view in the past and the same place in the 1980s..

Toker, Franklin **Pittsburgh: An Urban Portrait**. Pittsburgh: University of Pittsburgh Press,1986. This architect professor mines news accounts and old records to present in small geographical sections, a cultural and architectural history of Pittsburgh.

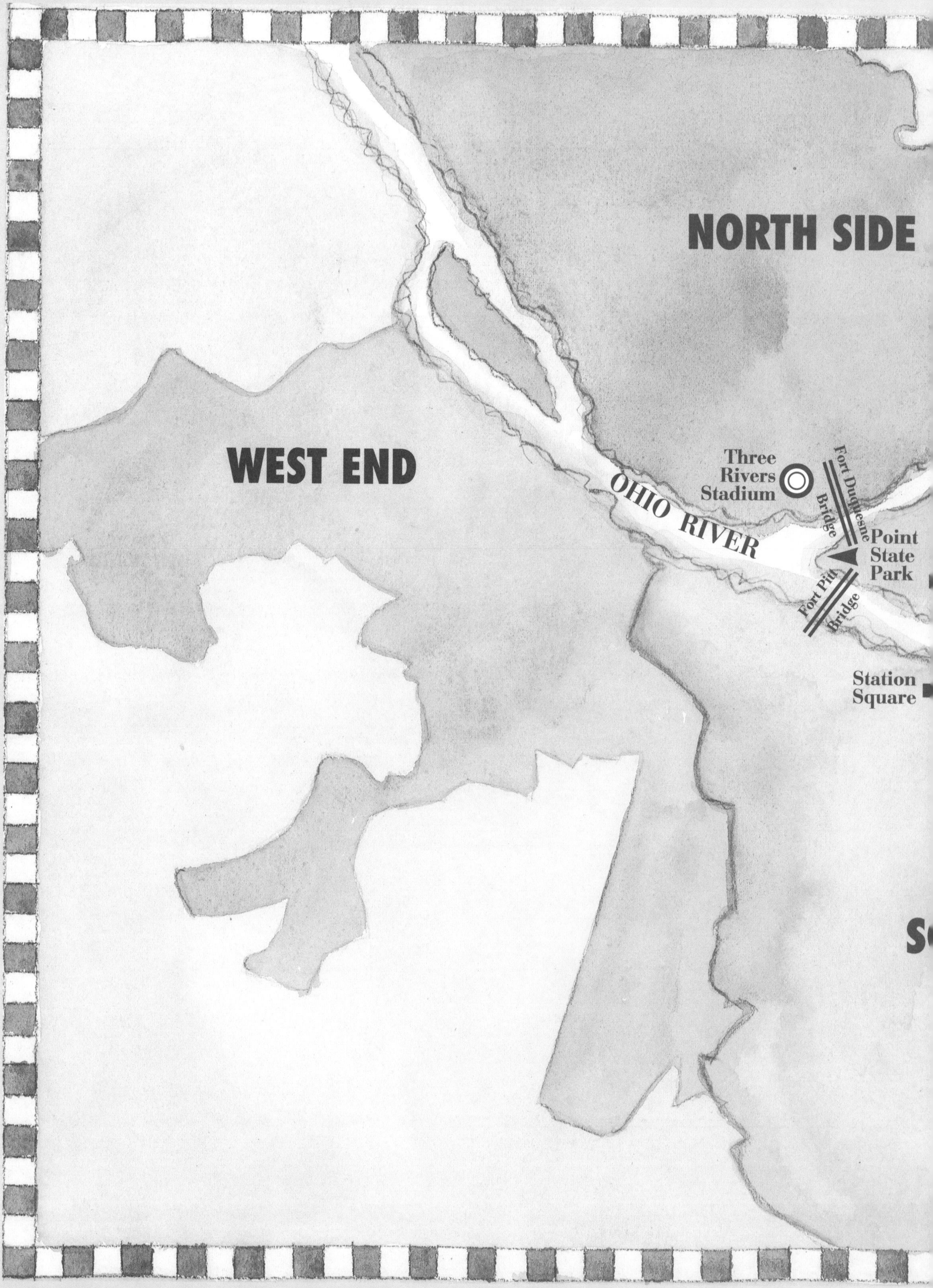

NORTH SIDE

WEST END

OHIO RIVER

Three
Rivers
Stadium

Fort Duquesne
Bridge

Point
State
Park

Fort Pitt
Bridge

Station
Square

So